THE HUMAN BEHIND THE HERO

BREC BASSINGER IS STARGIRL®

HOT TOPICS

KRISTEN RAJCZAK NELSON

Gareth Stevens PUBLISHING

Please visit our website, www.garethstevens.com. For a free color catalog of all our high-quality books, call toll free 1-800-542-2595 or fax 1-877-542-2596.

Library of Congresss Cataloging-in-Publication Data
Names: Rajczak Nelson, Kristen, author.
Title: Brec Bassinger is Stargirl / Kristen Rajczak Nelson.
Description: Buffalo, New York : Gareth Stevens Publishing, [2023] | Series: The human behind the hero | Includes index.
Identifiers: LCCN 2022018032 (print) | LCCN 2022018033 (ebook) | ISBN 9781538283752 (paperback) | ISBN 9781538283776 (library binding) | ISBN 9781538283783 (ebook)
Subjects: LCSH: Bassinger, Brec, 1999–Juvenile literature. | Television actors and actresses–United States–Biography–Juvenile literature. | Stargirl (Fictitious character)–Juvenile literature.
Classification: LCC PN2287.B3846 R35 2023 (print) | LCC PN2287.B3846 (ebook) | DDC 792.4502/8092 [B]–dc23/eng/20220418
LC record available at https://lccn.loc.gov/2022018032
LC ebook record available at https://lccn.loc.gov/2022018033

First Edition

Published in 2023 by
Gareth Stevens Publishing
2544 Clinton St
Buffalo, NY 14224

Designer: Rachel Rising
Editor: Kristen Nelson

Photo credits: Cover, pp. 1, 5, 17, 29 Kathy Hutchins/Shutterstock.com; Cover, pp. 1-32 KID_A/Shutterstock.com; Cover, pp. 1-32 gn8/Shutterstock.com; p. 7 https://commons.wikimedia.org/wiki/File:Brec_Bassinger_HHH_2015.jpg; p. 9 logoboom/Shutterstock.com; p. 11 WENN Rights Ltd / Alamy Stock Photo; pp. 13, 21 Featureflash Photo Agency/Shutterstock.com; p. 15 INTERFOTO / Personalities/Alamy Stock Photo; pp .19 DFree/Shutterstock.com; p. 23, 25 Album / Alamy Stock Photo; p. 27 Tinseltown/Shutterstock.com.

Printed in the United States of America

CPSIA compliance information: Batch #CWGS23: For further information contact Gareth Stevens, New York, New York at 1-800-542-2595.

CONTENTS

Soon to Be a Star! 4
California, Here She Comes 8
Brec Is Bella 12
It's in the Stars 16
Time to Prepare 20
The Supersuit 22
The Long Shoot 24
More Seasons 26
What Does the Future Hold? 28
Timeline 30
For More Information 31
Glossary 32
Index 32

SOON TO BE A STAR!

Brec Bassinger is better known as Stargirl now, but she started out as a kid with a big dream. Brec was born on May 25, 1999, in Saginaw, Texas. She has two older brothers, Beric and Brice.

BEHIND THE SCENES

BREC LIKES SPORTS! SHE PLAYED VOLLEYBALL AND OTHER SPORTS AND DID CHEERLEADING.

Brec first stepped into the spotlight in **pageants** starting at age two. One of the pageant judges asked her to be in a movie he was making. She loved it! Brec started taking classes at an acting school.

BEHIND THE SCENES

IN 2009, BREC WON THE TITLE OF WORLD'S OUR LITTLE MISS IN A PAGEANT.

CALIFORNIA, HERE SHE COMES

Brec went to Los Angeles, California, and started **auditioning**. Her mom went with her. Her first TV appearance was on *The Goldbergs* in 2013. Soon after, Brec got her first big part. She and her mom moved to Los Angeles!

BEHIND THE SCENES

BREC WOULD APPEAR ON *THE GOLDBERGS* AGAIN IN 2016 AS THE SAME CHARACTER.

Brec appeared on the Nickelodeon TV show *The Haunted Hathaways.* She played Emma Hawking, a member of the gymnastics team on the show. Brec's sports background was helping her get parts!

BEHIND THE SCENES

AT FIRST, BREC WAS SUPPOSED TO JUST BE ON ONE EPISODE OF *THE HAUNTED HATHAWAYS*. SHE ENDED UP PLAYING EMMA IN 10 EPISODES!

BREC IS BELLA

In 2015, Brec got her big break. She was cast as Bella Dawson on the Nickelodeon show *Bella and the Bulldogs.* She played a middle school girl who becomes the quarterback of the school football team.

BEHIND THE SCENES

BREC ALSO STARRED IN A NICKELODEON MOVIE CALLED *LIAR, LIAR, VAMPIRE* IN 2015.

To prepare for the part of Bella, Brec went to football camp for two weeks. She worked on playing football but also really looking the part: "The **persona** that a quarterback has on the field, the way they walk and talk is very confident."

BEHIND THE SCENES

BREC DIDN'T GET TACKLED ON *BELLA AND THE BULLDOGS*—BUT BELLA DID! BREC HAD A STUNT DOUBLE WHO TOOK THE HITS.

IT'S IN THE STARS

Bella and the Bulldogs ended after two seasons. Then Brec was back to auditioning for parts. She appeared on the shows *All Night* and *School of Rock*. She also tried out for the part of a superhero named Starlight and a movie called *Stargirl*!

BEHIND THE SCENES

BREC HAS SAID: "I GREW UP LOVING SUPERHERO MOVIES, ABSOLUTELY LOVED THEM."

In 2018, Brec started auditioning for *DC's Stargirl*, the TV show she would star in. It was very secretive. She did know she was trying out to play Courtney Whitmore. Courtney is a high school student who finds a **cosmic** staff and becomes a superhero!

BEHIND THE SCENES

STARGIRL IS BASED ON A COMIC BOOK CHARACTER. THE FIRST TIME SHE APPEARED IN A COMIC WAS IN MAY 1999—THE MONTH AND YEAR BREC WAS BORN!

TIME TO PREPARE

Once Brec knew she got the part, she read comics featuring Stargirl to prepare. She also learned to fight with the cosmic staff, which was much taller than her. Brec was already good at the gymnastics her character would need to do!

BEHIND THE SCENES

BREC'S MOM IS OFTEN ON SET WHEN BREC IS WORKING. THEY ARE VERY CLOSE!

THE SUPERSUIT

Preparing for *Stargirl* meant more than 15 costume fittings for Brec. The Stargirl supersuit was made especially for her. Brec said: "Every time I put on that supersuit, I do feel more like a superhero. It was a great acting tool to have with me."

BEHIND THE SCENES

BREC WAS HAPPY WITH HER STARGIRL COSTUME PARTLY BECAUSE IT WAS HOT WHILE FILMING IN ATLANTA, GEORGIA. HER CASTMATES' COSTUMES MADE THEM SWEAT MORE!

THE LONG SHOOT

Brec and the cast of *Stargirl* spent eight months in Atlanta filming the first season of the show. She had a stunt double. But Brec also learned how to do some stunts. As filming continued, she got to do more and more!

BEHIND THE SCENES

BREC HAS TYPE 1 DIABETES. THIS MAKES THE LONG HOURS OF FILMING VERY HARD ON HER BODY SOMETIMES.

MORE SEASONS

Stargirl premiered on May 18, 2020. Fans loved it! The show earned a second season, which started airing in August 2021. Brec was a becoming a star as Stargirl! She started to get ready for season three.

BEHIND THE SCENES

BREC LOVES ACTING, BUT SHE'S ALSO INTERESTED IN WRITING AND DIRECTING.

WHAT DOES THE FUTURE HOLD?

Brec Bassinger was only about 13 when she first went to Los Angeles. She was about to turn 21 when *Stargirl* began to air. Her success has come early, but it's been earned. With hard work and a dream, for Brec, the stars are the limit!

BEHIND THE SCENES

BREC HAS USED HER YOUTUBE CHANNEL TO TALK TO HER FANS AND PRACTICE MAKING HER OWN VIDEOS!

TIMELINE

1999 BREC BASSINGER IS BORN ON MAY 25.

2013 SHE FIRST APPEARS ON TV ON *THE GOLDBERGS* AND *THE HAUNTED HATHAWAYS.*

2015 BREC STARS AS BELLA DAWSON ON *BELLA AND THE BULLDOGS.*

2016 THE LAST EPISODE OF *BELLA AND THE BULLDOGS* AIRS ON JUNE 25. BREC BEGINS APPEARING ON *SCHOOL OF ROCK.*

2018 BREC APPEARS ON THE SHOW *ALL NIGHT.* SHE IS CAST AS STARGIRL/COURTNEY WHITMORE IN *DC'S STARGIRL.*

2020 *STARGIRL* PREMIERES ON MAY 18.

2021 *STARGIRL'S* SECOND SEASON BEGINS AIRING ON AUGUST 10.

FOR MORE INFORMATION

BOOKS

Johns, Geoff. *Stargirl*. Burbank, CA: DC Comics, 2020.

Marsham, Liz, et al. *DC: Absolutely Everything You Need to Know*. New York, NY: DK Publishing, 2018.

WEBSITES

Brec Bassinger – IMDB
www.imdb.com/name/nm5561229/
Follow Brec's career on the Internet Movie Database.

DC's Stargirl Official Site
www.cwtv.com/shows/stargirl
Check out *Stargirl* here!

Stargirl—DC
www.dccomics.com/characters/stargirl
Read more about the character Stargirl on the official DC website.

Publisher's note to educators and parents: Our editors have carefully reviewed these websites to ensure that they are suitable for students. Many websites change frequently, however, and we cannot guarantee that a site's future contents will continue to meet our high standards of quality and educational value. Be advised that students should be closely supervised whenever they access the internet.

GLOSSARY

audition: To try out for.

cosmic: Having to do with outer space or the universe.

episode: A TV show that is one part of a series.

pageant: Beauty and talent contest.

persona: The way someone talks or acts around others.

stunt double: A person who takes an actor's place during the filming of stunts and dangerous scenes for a movie or TV show.

tackle: To grab a player and throw them to the ground.

type 1 diabetes: A disorder that causes the body to produce too much urine and causes high levels of sugar in the blood. Those with type 1 diabetes often find out when they are young.

INDEX

Atlanta, Georgia, 23, 24
Bella and the Bulldogs, 12, 14, 15, 16
comic book, 19, 20
costume, 22, 23
DC's Stargirl, 18, 19, 22, 24, 26, 28
diabetes, 25
family, 4, 8, 21
Haunted Hathaways, The, 10, 11
Los Angeles, California, 8, 28
pageants, 6, 7
sports, 5, 10, 20
stunts, 15, 24
Texas, 4